929.4

# The Story of Surnames

Lilian Devereux

*Illustrated by Ian Escott*

Basil Blackwell                                                    Oxford

631 10880 7

Printed in Great Britain by Billing & Sons Ltd, Guildford
and bound by the Kemp Hall Bindery, Oxford

# Introduction

We all have two kinds of name; first we have our own personal names or Christian names, then we have the name we share with the members of our family. We call this our surname.

Many, many years ago, when people lived in small groups, only personal names were needed. But as the years went by, the population of the country increased, and the small hamlets grew into villages, and the villages became towns, and when there were a number of people with the same name, it became necessary to distinguish one from another. So other names were added and surnames gradually came into use and in the thirteenth and fourteenth centuries became general.

You know that the thirteenth and fourteenth centuries mean from the year 1200 to the year 1400.

There are four main groups of surnames. They are— names showing relationship, names showing occupations or jobs, describing names or nicknames and place names.

We also have many surnames which came from foreign languages, but we will talk about those at the end of the book.

# Names Formed from Relationships

Perhaps the easiest way to distinguish the person you were talking about was to say, "Dick, who is John's son", and there you are, Dick Johnson. Think of all the names ending with 'son' that you know, Williamson, Richardson, Stephenson or Stevenson, Davidson, and many others that you will find yourself.

Very few people could write in early days, and when they could they did not worry about spelling. Very often, too, the clerks, or writers, either did not listen carefully, or were just careless and wrote the names in different ways. Dickson might be written as Dixon, Adamson could become Addison, Andrewson be changed to Anderson, while Matthewson could easily become Mathieson.

Simpson is the son of Simon or Simeon and Ferguson the son of Fergus.

Shortened names were often instead of the full name and they made another lot of surnames. For instance, from the name Daniel we get Danielson and Daniels, but from the short form Dan, we also get Danns and Danson.

John is the most common Christian name in our country and it is found in various forms all over Europe. Ian, Sean, Evan, Hans, Jean, Juan, Jan and Ivan are some of the variants of John. From John and the nicknames Jack and Jan we can get many surnames including Johns, Jones, Johnson, Jacks, Jackson, Jake, Jakes and Janson.

Richard had a lot of short forms, Rick, Dick, Dickon and Diccon, Hich, Rich, Digg, Hig, Hitch were some of them. 'Son' added to all these give many more well known names, Dickson or Dixon, Rickson and many others.

*Simon and Simpson*

2

The name Hugh also became altered in many strange ways, some of them being Hug, Huggin, Huggett, Hitchin, Hewitt, Hewlett and Howett and even Hud. Some of the sons' names would be Hewson, Hudson, Hughes and Hewitson.

An older word meaning 'son of' was 'ing' and sometimes both endings were used together in such names as Higgingson and Hutchinson.

You know that duckling and gosling mean little duck and a little goose and that pigling means a little pig. In the same way, 'kin', 'et', or 'ett', at the end of a name means little or dear little. Dickin or Dickon meant little Dick. A short form of Bartholomew is Bart, so Bartlett could mean little Bartholomew. Jenkin means little John, his son would be Jenkinson or Jennings. Peterkin, Perkin or Parkin all mean little Peter and we get the names Perkinson and Parkinson. Pierre, the French for Peter became Piers or Pearce, giving us the name Pearson.

Bennett is probably little Ben and his son is Benson, while Gregson could be the son of Gregory.

A short form of Walter is Wat and so we get Watson.

Colin is a nickname for Nicholas and we find Colinson, Wilson is Will's son, Wilkinson means the son of little Will, and Tomlinson is the son of dear little Tom. A short name used for Robert was Rob, others were Robin and Hob, and so the names Hobson, Robson and Robinson grew up. Olaf's son might be called Olson.

Henry is often called Harry, this gives us Harrison. Hanson could be the son of Hans and Dennison the son of Dennis.

The same form is used in other countries. In Scandinavia we see the names Larson, Neilson and Ericson. The Normans used the word Fitz, meaning 'son,' and from this

3

we get the names Fitzgerald, Fitzalan, Fitzpatrick and others.

In Welsh, Ap or Ab means 'son'. Ap Rees, which means the son of the king, became Preece, Price or Brice, Ap Richard turned into Prichard or Pritchard, Ab Lud changed to Blood, while Ab Owen and Ab Evan became Bowen and Bevan.

The 'Mac' in Scottish names is also 'son', and gives us names like MacDonald, son of the world ruler, MacGregor and MacPherson. This last name means the son of the parson. MacGowan is the son of the smith, MacIntyre the son of the carpenter. MacDougall, MacDugold and MacDowell are versions of the same name meaning the son of the dark stranger, that is, the son of the Dane.

Another word ending meaning small is 'ock'. A bullock is a small bull, a hillock a small hill. Little Paul was Paulock which has come down to us as Pollock.

A son might also be distinguished from his father by being called young John, and this later became John Young.

*MacGowan*

## Surnames from the Mother's Names

You will have noticed that all the names we have examined so far, came from the fathers' names, but there are some which developed from the name of the mother.

Margerison and Marjerson may be from the son of Margery, while Margotson could come from Margaret who was called Margot for short.

A fairly common name for a woman was Gillian (Jill for short) from which we get names beginning with Gill: Gills, Gillott, Gillett, Gilpin, Gilliand and Gilmour are a few.

4

Godeve may come from the well-known name Godiva; Beatie, Betts, Bettinson, Bettison and Betony may come from Beatrice; Sisson and Sisley from Cecilia and Ibbotson from Ib, which is a nickname for Isabella. A girl called Matilda is often known as Tilda or Tilly, so we get the names Tillotson, Tildey, Tildeson, Tillson, Tillett and Tilney, while Joyson seems to be Joyce's son.

The old words sib and kin mean relations, and these may give us the surnames Sibson and Kinson.

A group of names was made by using personal names without any extra ending as surnames. Examples are Cuthbert, changed sometimes to Cobbett, Gilbert, Hammond, Howard, Hubert or Hibbert, Neil, from Nigel, Neville, Harvey, Stanley, Percy and Mayhew, for Matthew. Gibbon comes from Gib, short for Gilbert, and it also gives us Gibbs and Gibson. Other names used like this are Douglas, Clifford, Lewis, Lawrence and Oliver. Now fashion has changed again and these are very popular Christian names once more.

*Lord Nelson*

## Famous Names

Let us look at a few famous names which were formed from relationships.

One of the most famous names in our history is that of Lord Nelson. He was our greatest sailor who defeated Napoleon's fleet in three great battles. They were the Battle of the Nile, the Battle of the Baltic and the Battle of Trafalgar. The name comes from Nell's son.

Ben Jonson (another spelling of John's son) was a fine poet and playwright who lived at the same time as Shakespeare.

Have you read that exciting story, *Treasure Island*? If so,

5

*George Stephenson*

you know it was written by Robert Louis Stevenson. Perhaps you know some of his other books and also his poems called *A Child's Garden of Verse*.

George Stephenson was famous as the inventor of the steam locomotive called the *Rocket*. It was not the first one made, but it was the most successful.

James Watt also made steam engines first used for pumping and later for working machinery. The cylinders of his engines were made by an ironfounder called John Wilkinson.

Macadam (son of Adam) was a Scotsman who, in the early nineteenth century invented a way to improve roads. He made them of layers of stone, usually granite, and we call them macadamised roads.

William Harvey, who lived in Charles I's time, was a doctor who discovered the way the blood circulates in our bodies.

Sir Philip Sidney was a brave soldier and also a poet. He lived in Queen Elizabeth I's reign. Perhaps you have read the story of how he lay severely wounded after a battle and one of his men brought him a cup of water. But he refused it and gave it to a soldier lying nearby, saying, "Your need is greater than mine."

Robert Browning and his wife Elizabeth Barret Browning were both poets. One of Browning's poems you may know is *The Pied Piper of Hamelin*. The name means the son of the brown-haired man.

John Bunyan was a tinker of Bedford. He was imprisoned because he went about preaching, and in those days only priests were allowed to preach. Bunyan wrote the book *Pilgrim's Progress*, a book which is read all over the world. The name Bunyan comes from an old Welsh name Ap or Ab Annian.

*John Bunyan*

6

Henry Hudson was one of the explorers who tried to find the North-West Passage. He found the bay now called Hudson's Bay but his men mutinied. Hudson and his son were put into a small boat and were never seen again.

Edward Gibbon was a great historian, perhaps our greatest. His best work was a book about the Roman Empire.

Admiral Jellicoe was an English admiral during the 1914–18 war. His name came from a pet name for Gillian.

## Puzzles for You

Here are three names for you to work out yourself.

1. He was a great writer who lived in the eighteenth century. Though he wrote many books he is best known for his dictionary. A friend of his wrote a book about his life. If you live in, or have visited the lovely city of Lichfield you will find this easy.

The name of this man was S - - - - - J - - - - - -.

S - - - - - J - - - - - -

2. She helped a prince who was fleeing from his enemies, by disguising him as her servant and taking him in a boat over the sea to an island.

Her name was F - - - - M - - - - - - - -, and the prince she saved was—whom?

3. This man was a remarkable inventor. He was interested in electricity, the telegraph and telephone and made many improvements in them. He invented the phonograph, the fore-runner of our gramophone, and worked on what were at that time called "Moving Pictures".

He was T - - - - - E - - - - -.

How many more names in this group can you find?

7

# Occupational Names

*Cobbler*

In the early days there were no shops and stores as we have now. People had to depend on themselves for everything they needed to eat, wear and use.

Most villages consisted of a castle or a large manor house occupied by the lord of the village, a church, the priest's house and a number of huts where the serfs, or peasants lived. The serfs had to work in the fields or the castle for the lord, work the priest's field and they had strips of land in which they grew their own crops.

In the castle were many servants and workers, among them would be a blacksmith. He would not only shoe the horses but make armour, axle pins for waggons, fish hooks and carriage wheels. Spits for roasting meat would be made by him too. Bread was baked by the baker, cooks and scullions worked in the kitchen preparing the food for the household. The cobbler made and repaired shoes and also made leather purses and bottles for wine, as glass was, as yet, unknown.

The dairymaid made cheese in the dairy. She was called the dey, which perhaps gives us the surname Day.

As well as the cultivated fields there was also some common land. This belonged to all the people and they used it to pasture their cattle and geese. They could cut turf for fuel and take wood for their fires or for furniture from this land.

When the corn was reaped and threshed it was taken to the miller who ground it in his mill. It might be a windmill or a water mill driven by a wheel turned by a stream or river. Sometimes one mill would serve a number of small

*Miller*

*Archer*

*Shepherd*

villages, larger villages and towns would have their own.

So you can understand why such a lot of names are formed from occupations. It was easy to say John the smith, Thomas the baker, or Hal the mason, and so we got John Smith, Thomas Baker and Hal Mason. You will be able to think of many more for yourself, but I'll tell you some of the less familiar ones. Many of the occupations once very common are not now in existence, but we can remember them from surnames still in use.

Archer or Bowman are easy, but Baxter is harder. It is an old name for a bakehouse and so means much the same as Baker. A cross-bowman was Arblaster or Balestier, the latter name has become altered to Banister.

A favourite sport of the kings and their courtiers was hunting deer and wild boar in the forests. They also hunted wild fowl with trained hawks and falcons. They kept many servants to look after their horses, hounds and falcons. The Falconer looked after the falcons and other birds used in the chase; sometimes this name is spelt Faulkner. Fowler, Groom, Hawker, Shepherd, Herd, Hunter and Hunt, Gardener or Gardner are plain, but have you heard of Todhunter? Tod was an old name for a fox, and it is still used in Scotland. Foxes, of course, did a lot of damage among the villagers' ducks and geese. Todhunter who hunted them, was paid by the village warden for each one he killed.

If cattle or other farm animals got loose and wandered about in the fields of crops they could damage them. So the Pinder, or Pinner, rounded up stray animals and shut them in the village pound until they were claimed by the owners. The name Pinfold also comes from an enclosure or pound used for straying animals.

A Cooper made the iron hoops which hold barrels

9

*Joiner*

*Palmer*

together, a Salter made salt, a Turner turned (that is, shaped) wooden articles on a lathe, Bateman was probably a boatman, a Cutler made or sold knives, spoons and combs were made of horn by a Horner. A Fletcher made arrows, sometimes this is spelt Flecher or Flecker. A Joiner was a carpenter, another spelling is Joyner. Panter or Pantler was the chief servant in charge of the food; now you will think of the word pantry.

A Pitcher filled the spaces between boards in a boat with pitch. Bark from trees was used in tanning leather and we get Barker and Tanner. Carver, Leadbeater, Goldsmith, Potter and Reaper, or Ripper, and Waterman are plain, and so is Plowman. Copestake, or Capstick, was a woodcutter, and a Chandler made and sold candles. You can still see chandlers' shops.

In the Middle Ages many men thought it a good act to make a pilgrimage to a holy place. Some used to go to the shrine of Thomas à Becket, but more went to the Holy Land. They often travelled on foot and suffered great hardships, and of course it took years to accomplish their pilgrimage. A Palmer was a man who had done this, and he wore a cockle shell to show where he had been. Another old English name for a pilgrim was Wade.

When churches and houses were built, the inside was decorated with stain or paint by the Painter and Stainer.

You have read in your History books of monasteries where monks lived, and of friars who travelled about preaching. They may have given us the surnames Monk, Prior and Friar, and perhaps Fryor is another spelling for the latter. Deacon, too, is a name from a churchman.

The name Jenner came from engineer. This did not mean the same as it does now. An engineer made gins, that is, snares or traps. A Shoesmith was what we call a Blacksmith,

10

the names can still be seen over a forge. Another name for him was Farrier, often changed to Ferrier or Farrar. We talk of waits who sing carols at Christmas time, but the word originally meant a watchman and gives us the names Waite and Waites.

A Forester looked after the woods and forests, a gamekeeper was known as a Warrener; these names have become Forster, Foster and Warner or Warren.

Marner came from a mariner or sailor. A very old name for a fiddle, which is no longer used, was a crowd. From this we get the name Crowther, though we also have Fiddler. A Massinger was a messenger.

A park-keeper was called Parker, a Lorimer or Loriner made straps for harness. A Lander or Launder was a washerman or washerwoman, you will notice the resemblance to the word laundry.

A Reeder thatched roofs with reeds, a Fuller cleaned or bleached cloth, a Tozer 'teased' or combed out the fibres of flax or wool when making cloth. The seed heads of the plant called Teasels were used to do this. A Shearman cut off the rough threads from the cloth with shears.

A Slater cut and shaped slates and an Ostler, or Hostler, looked after the horses at an inn.

The lord of the village was often cruel and harsh and so had many enemies. So, in case anyone tried to poison him, he had a servant called the Sewer. It was this man's job to serve up the meals at the lord's table and to taste the food first. If the poor sewer seemed well after the tasting, there was no poison in the food and the lord was able to eat his meal in comfort.

Before wine and ale became common a drink called mead was made from honey. Perhaps the name Meade came from the maker of this drink.

*Lord with Sewer*

As well as cooking, cleaning and helping in the fields the women and girls spun wool and flax into yarn. Sometimes they wove it into cloth at home, or they might take it to the village Weaver. If the village was too small to have a weaver living in it a travelling one would visit it once or twice a year and stay there until he had woven all the yarn. The women then had to make the cloth into garments.

The housewives must have been glad to receive a visit from the Pedlar who sold pins and needles, laces and ribbons, strings of beads and perfume. Some pedlars had the reputation of being dishonest. In one of Shakespeare's plays, a pedlar appears who says that he is a 'snapper-up of unconsidered trifles', which means that he was ready to steal anything he could find. Chapman and Packman are other names for a pedlar.

Later on, markets were started where the villagers and farmers could take their produce and exchange it for something else they needed.

Later still the great annual fairs were established. They were like very large markets and sometimes lasted for days or even weeks. In many places these old fairs still survive. We hear of Goose fairs, Cherry fairs and so on, but they are generally only places for amusement now.

At markets and fairs goods are displayed on booths, or stalls. Quite likely the modern name Booth came from a man who made booths, or owned one at the fair.

A very common name is Ward and it means a keeper or guard. Durward was a door-ward and you can tell at once what Woodward means. Hayward was a hedge-ward, and is sometimes Howard or Hereward. The old word hay, meaning a hedge, also gives us Hay, Haig and Haigh.

A cowherd looked after the cows, it is sometimes Coward, and Lambert might have come from the lamb-herd.

The sty-ward looked after the pigs, but this name later became Steward, an official, and later still Stuart was the family name of the kings of Scotland and gained in importance.

Other names which have increased in importance are Constable, once meaning stable fellow, and Marshall meaning much the same as Constable. A Sergeant once meant a servant and Governor was a steersman. An Usher was a doorkeeper, or porter, and from this we get the names Lush and Lusher.

Rouncey was an old name for a nag (or horse) and the name Runciman was the person in charge of the rouncies or runcies. If you have read about Don Quixote you will remember that his horse was called Rocinante, which comes from the same word family.

*Runciman*

13

*Scribe*

Sherman, Skurmer, Skirmer or Shurmer mean a swordsman or fencer, and Souter was another name for a cobbler. A Waller built walls, Skinner and Porter are easy. Bond or Band was a farmer or householder, from which come Husband and Younghusband. Faraday, or Ferriday, was a labourer who travelled about the country working at farms where help was needed. A Crocker, or Croker, sold pottery, a scribe, or writer, could be called Scriven or Scrivener. The name Patten comes from the maker of pattens which were wooden shoes worn in wet weather.

An old name for a rabbit, we find it in the Bible, is coney, so the names Coney, Conie or Cony, could be either nicknames, or mean dealers in rabbit skins. Deatheridge was a tinder maker, a Lister was a dyer, a Thrower wound silk. A Whittier dressed (or prepared) white leather and a Pavier paved walks and floors.

We talk of foundries, a Founder cast bells or cannon in iron.

Some names have 'ster' at the end, it means the same as 'we'. We can have Brewer or Brewster, Webber or Webster and these two mean the same as Weaver. A Dempster was a judge and this title is still used in the Isle of Man.

Some more easy names are Piper, Sadler, Seaman, Shearer, Fisher, Hornblower, Harper and Thatcher.

Linsey was a cloth made of wool and linen, a Mercer was a man who sold cloth. A Hind was a farm servant. A Page was a boy training to be a knight, Pagett could be a little page. After being a page for some time the boy became a Squire and accompanied a knight into battle. If he proved himself worthy and brave he was made a knight himself.

When a boy wanted to learn a trade he had to become an apprentice for seven years. During that time he lived in his master's house and worked there, learning his job. At the end of his apprenticeship he had to prove that he had learnt his craft well by making some shoes if he was going to be a shoemaker, gloves if a glover, a piece of furniture if a joiner and so on. If he passed this test he became a journeyman and could set up his own shop and teach other boys. Probably the names Prentice and Prentiss come from the word apprentice. Do you remember the story of Dick Whittington who was an apprentice to a merchant?

The name Kings could mean a king's man, that is, a man who was a servant of the king, and Priests or Priestman would be the priest's man.

Servants and apprentices were known by their masters' names, so Johns, Richards, Adams, Gills, Harris would mean John's man, Richard's man, Harry's man and so on. You have noticed by now how often the letters 'y' and 'i' are interchanged.

The name Merryman was probably a jester. It was customary for kings and other wealthy people to keep a jester in their household. This man, who was sometimes a dwarf or a hunchback, had to keep his master and his friends always amused. The jester usually wore clothes made of two colours, for example, half would be red and half yellow. He carried a stick with bells or a bladder on the end and wore a pointed hat, often decorated with bells.

However unhappy or ill the jester felt, jokes and jests had to be made and if he was not very funny, or the guests didn't laugh enough, the poor fellow was punished.

A name we often see is Wright. A wright was a man who wrought, that is, worked. A Shipwright made ships, a Cartwright carts, and as you know, Shakespeare was a playwright. A wagon was called a wain, and we have the

*Jester*

*Charcoal Burner*

*Teller*

names Wain, Wayne and Wainwright. Arkwright made arks, which were bins, Goodwright should surely be a good, skilful worker, and Cheesewright is obvious. A Wheelwright and Plo-wright made—what?

An interesting name is Ashbolt. Bolt or boult means to sift. Did he perhaps sift the ashes, working with charcoal burners in the forest? The name Ashburner also must come from the old days of charcoal burning. Coleman and Collier also mean a charcoal burner. However, as some cabbages are called kale or cole, Coleman might also mean a man who grew or sold cabbages.

A Reeve was a steward or an important officer. One in charge of a port was the Portreeve and the Woodreeve was what we should call a gamekeeper. The land was divided into shires, the officer in charge of a shire was the Shirereeve, and so we get Sheriff.

A Chanter was a singer, while a Chamberlain was an official in the household of a king or a nobleman. A man who was good at sports, archery or running, or who defended a cause, or fought in single combat for himself or on someone else's behalf, was a Champion.

The verb 'to tell' used to mean 'to count'. The full number was the 'tally' or the 'tale', while the man who counted was the 'teller'. This word is still used. We read in the Bible that Pharaoh commanded that though the Israelite slaves were not given any straw they yet had to make the same 'tale' of bricks. Names from this word are Tallis and Tellis.

In the Middle Ages many men were serfs; they were almost slaves and could not change their masters without permission. In those days Freeman was a proud name. It belonged to someone who was not a serf, or who had been freed from serfdom. Franklin, Yeoman and Burgess were

16

also free men who owned their land and did not owe service to the lord of the manor. A churl, too, was free, and he was entitled to hold thirty acres of land.

In 1381 the peasants rebelled against their oppressors and the unjust taxes. They armed themselves with axes, farm implements and old arrows and swords. The leader of one group from Essex called himself Jack Straw. The men from Kent were led by Wat the Tyler, that is, Walter Tyler, or Tiler, who made tiles. The king, Richard II, then only fifteen years old, rode out to meet these fierce men and promised to improve their lot and pardoned them.

But though he gave them letters granting them their freedom, his promises were never carried out and later many of the poor country people were tortured and killed.

It was not until the eighteenth century that turnips were widely grown and used as winter food for cattle. Until then, most of the cattle and sheep were killed at the beginning of winter and the flesh was salted. This was the only method of preserving meat and it was by no means as good as our modern ways of canning and freezing. The salt meat was used all through the winter and early spring, and was often not very pleasant to taste. So many spices were used in preparing it to improve the flavour. The spices were bought from the Spicer.

How many more occupational names can you find?

## An Odd Group of Names

When so few people could read or write, they were especially fond of plays and dramas. The priests found that a good way to teach their people was by plays. Stories from the Bible were acted in the churches and were easily understood. Sometimes the play taught lessons of goodness,

kindness, honesty and other virtues. These were called Mystery Plays.

If a man acted well in a play or a pageant, the name of the character he took might be given to him, perhaps in fun at first, but it often stuck and so we find names like Pope, Cardinal, Bishop, Abbott, Prince, Knight, Baron or Lord.

How many more of these names can you find?

## Famous Names

Here are just a few of the famous names in this group.

Oliver Goldsmith was a writer who lived in the eighteenth century and was a friend of Doctor Johnson. His best known works are a book called *The Vicar of Wakefield* and an amusing play *She Stoops to Conquer*.

Two English composers were Sir John Stainer (1840–1901) and Thomas Tallis (1515–1585). Both these men wrote a lot of church music.

Joseph Turner (1775–1851) and John Constable (1776–1837) were two great English artists. Turner's pictures were full of wonderful colour. John Constable lived in Suffolk and loved to paint the scenes of sea, river, and countryside he saw around him.

Sir John Franklin was an explorer but in his early days he served in the Navy under Lord Nelson.

Richard Arkwright and Edmund Cartwright were two inventors who lived during the Industrial Revolution, that is the time when new methods and machines were being developed. Arkwright made spinning machines and Cartwright made looms.

Edmund Spenser was a poet who lived in Elizabeth's reign. His name comes from the 'dispenser' who dispensed, or gave out, the food and drink in the household of the lord at the castle.

Lord Lister (1827–1912) was a British surgeon who first discovered the use of antiseptics. This was a very important advance in medical knowledge for until then many people died, not from their wounds, but from infection.

Elizabeth Fry was a courageous woman who went alone into the terrible prisons which were so bad that the prison governors would not enter them. She found the prisoners

*Lord Lister*

19

almost starving, dirty, without beds or proper clothes, and quite neglected. She spent her life improving the conditions not only in prisons but also in hospitals and persuaded many other people to help in this work. Her name means 'free'.

In 1903 two American brothers called Orville and Wilbur Wright were the first men to fly successfully and in a machine they had made themselves. I need not tell you more about them, you will have read all about their adventure.

## Puzzles for You

Now for your puzzles.

1. This man was a sailor who was captain of a ship called the *Endeavour* in which he sailed round New Zealand and visited Australia. He later discovered New Caledonia and the Sandwich Islands.

You know his name, it was J - - - - C - - -.

2. He was the leader of an expedition to the highest mountain in the world. It was in 1953, and I needn't tell you any more for you know his name is S - - J - - - H - - -.

3. This man loves music and is one of our greatest conductors. He especially likes to help boys and girls to enjoy music. You have seen him on your television screen. He is often called 'England's Ambassador of Music' for he travels all over the world to conduct orchestras.

He is S - - M - - - - - S - - - - - -.

You will find many more names to add to this list.

# Descriptive and Nicknames

Let us look now at names and nicknames which described their owners.

Perhaps you know someone who has reddish hair and so is called Ginger, or Carrots. The use of nicknames used to be very common, far more than it is now.

In our History books we can find a large number. Here are a few, find some more yourself.

You have heard of Ethelred the Unready. The name Unready comes from an old word meaning 'without plans'. When the Danes attacked, Ethelred had no plans for fighting them and was forced to give them money to stay away. And of course, they came back for more. Ethelred had a friend who was nicknamed 'the Grasper' because he was so greedy and wanted everything for himself. He was not a true friend, he deserted Ethelred when he thought he could do better for himself.

Ethelred's son Edmund was quite a different sort of person. He was brave and fought courageously against the Danes and his nickname was Ironside.

You have heard of King Canute. His father was called Forkbeard, you won't need to be told why.

Because Richard I was tall and strong and brave in battle, he was known as Richard the Lionheart, meaning he was as brave as a lion. His brother, John, was called Lackland because he lost lands in France previously held by English kings.

Three of the sons of William the Conqueror (and that's a nickname) had nicknames too. The elders, Robert, was called Curthose, which meant 'short legs'. William II, the

*King Canute*

21

*The Black Prince*

*Elizabeth I*

second son, was named Rufus, which means 'red' because he had a very red face. Henry I, another son who was king of England was a learned man. He had a good knowledge of Greek and Latin, and translated Aesop's Fables into French. So he was named Beauclerc, which was French for 'good scholar'.

A king of Scotland who lived at the same time as Henry I was Malcolm III, but was called Canmore, which meant Big Head.

Henry II used to wear a sprig of broom as a badge. The Latin name for this flower is *planta genista* and so all the kings from Henry II to Richard II used Plantagenet as a sort of family name.

Edward I had very long legs so he was named Longshanks, and you have all heard of the Black Prince who was so called because he wore black armour.

An Emperor of the Holy Roman Empire, a very important man and one of the leaders of the Third Crusade, was called Frederick Barbarossa. This name meant Red Beard.

A fine scholar who was Bishop of Lincoln during the reign of Henry III was called Grosseteste meaning Great Head.

In later years Elizabeth I was known as Good Queen Bess, a name given her by the people who loved and admired her.

More recently Queen Victoria was called Victoria the Good, and her son, Edward VII was the Peacemaker.

So you can see how usual it was to give nicknames even to very great people and you will not be surprised to find many surnames springing from this custom.

Simple examples are Long, which has also become Lang and Laing, Short, White (meaning fair), Black (meaning dark), Brown (brown-haired), Strong, Blunt (from blond), Fairfax (fax meant hair), Moody and Stout. Stout did not mean fat, it meant brave and valiant. We still speak of a stout fellow. Doughty, too, means strong and brave, but a person who was cowardly could be named Craven. Another similar pair of names is Girling meaning lionheart for a brave man, and Milsopp or Milksopp for a soft, timid one.

Other descriptive names are Broadhead, Fairhead, Whitehead and Weatherhead, which was originally Wetherhead and means shaped like a wether, or sheep. And what about Sheepshank? They weren't always complimentary when giving names and didn't mind hurting other people's feelings. A name now famous once meant 'ugly head'. That name is Kennedy.

Sometimes 'head' became changed to 'ett' at the end of names like Blackett, Hackett, Doggett and Duckett. A corbie is a raven and from this we get Corbett.

A thin, haggard person got the name Gaunt, someone who was fleet of foot was Lightfoot, Hare or, like one of King Canute's sons, Harefoot. But a clumsy, slow man would be known as Puddifoot. A strong man was perhaps the first to be called Armstrong. The name Welcombe means well combed, so its owner was a person whose hair was always tidy and who was neatly and elegantly dressed.

Have you read about Hereward the Wake, a man who refused to give in to William the Conqueror? His name Wake means watchful.

We often speak of a hoar frost meaning a white frost. The name Hoarlock was given to someone who had a white lock of hair. Another form of it is Horlick and Whitlock is like it and means white lock.

We use such expressions as 'as strong as an ox', 'as timid

23

as a hare', 'as quiet as a mouse', 'as cunning as a fox', in which we are comparing people to animals.

Our ancestors did the same and they were very quick to see resemblances between people and animals or birds.

A big, well built man might be called Bull, or Bullock, Fox would be the name of a cunning person and Lamb was a gentle one. We find the names Wolf or Wolfe, Colt, Doe, Steer and Hogg. Was he a very greedy boy? You can understand why this name was sometimes changed to Hodd.

Quick, darting movements or a high, shrill voice might suggest bird nicknames, which are indeed very plentiful.

A man who always dressed in black and walked with a waddling gait might remind people of a Crow, or a hoarse voice might give him that name. A small neat woman in brown clothes could get the name Wren.

A vain person who liked to swagger about in fine clothes was of course, Peacock. A sweet singer was Nightingale, Lark or Larkin. Other bird names are Pye (from a magpie), Crane, Dove, Finch, Hawk, Hawke and Hawkins. Daw, Dawe or Dawes are from jackdaw, and there are Bunting, Pigeon and Sparrow. You will find some others yourself. Gosling may be a bird name but it is more likely to be a form of Jocelyn.

Some of these animal names may have a different origin as you will see later in the book.

We sometimes say that someone who is hard and un-feeling is 'as hard as stone' or 'as cold as steel', and we have the surnames Stone and Steel. Flint, too, is a name applied to a hard-hearted person.

An old English word meaning harsh and cruel was 'stark'. The Anglo-Saxons said William the Conqueror was stark when he destroyed their houses and fields to make the New Forest to hunt in. This word gives us Starkey.

## Another Odd Group

Then there is a group of interesting names made up of a verb, or doing word, and a noun, or naming word. The most famous is, of course, Shakespeare, and this name as you may know was spelt in many different ways. There are similar names Wagstaff and Breakspeare. The last may have been given to the victor in a tournament.

People who gained such names as Lovejoy, Makepeace, Goodchild, Goodfellow, Goodman, Goodwill, Goodliffe, Trueman or Wiseman must have been very nice to know, but what of Dolittle? That sounds like a lazy creature, doesn't it?

Fairweather and Drinkwater are other names in this group, and so is Playfair which means playfellow. Goodbeer kept an inn where he sold strong, good liquor. Loveday was a day appointed for enemies to make up their quarrels and become friends again. It would be given as a name to a child born on that day.

Gotobed was a person who was fonder of sleeping than of work. It reminds us of the old Nursery Rhyme,

> 'To bed, to bed', says Sleepy-head,
> 'Tarry awhile', says Slow.

It could happen that members of the same family got different surnames. Let us think of a man called Robert who was a smith. He had three sons, Cederic, Ralph and Stephen.

The father would be known as Robert the smith, which would later become Robert Smith. His eldest son, Cedric, stayed at home to work with his father. He might be called Cedric the smith's son, or Cedric the son of Robert. So his surname eventually would be either Smithson or Robertson.

*Gotobed*

25

*Painter*

*Cardinal Wolsey*

The second son, Ralph, went to work at a neighbouring farm where he was known as Ralph, the new man, and in the end became Ralph Newman.

The third son, Stephen, went far away to a town where he learned the craft of painting and staining the walls in a new church that was being built. So his surname probably became Painter or Stainer.

So we have a father and three sons all with different names, a peculiar result.

**Famous Names**

John Bull was a composer and organist who lived from 1563 to 1628. He wrote a lot of music and it is believed that he composed our National Anthem.

Admiral Byrd was an American who was the first man to fly over the North and South Poles.

Cardinal Wolsey was an important churchman in the reign of Henry VIII. You can read in your History books how he and the king quarrelled. His name comes from 'wolf's eye'.

You have heard of Edmund Hillary who climbed Mount Everest. His name is from a Latin word meaning 'cheerful'.

Charles Lamb was a writer who wrote many books including some very famous essays. For children he wrote *Tales from Shakespeare*. His name suited him very well, for he was a kind and gentle man who devoted his life to looking after his sister who was ill.

Two poets in this group were Thomas Gray and John Gay. Gay was a Devonshire man and was a dramatist as well as a poet. He wrote *The Beggars' Opera*.

Lady Jane Grey was the unlucky girl who was queen for only nine days and was then beheaded.

One of the seamen of Devon who accompanied Sir Francis Drake on some of his exploits was Sir John Hawkins

Charles Darwin was a naturalist. He journeyed in the South Seas and astonished the whole world by his theory about the development of animals and plants. His name, from an old word, means 'dear friend'.

**Puzzles for You**

1. She brought help and comfort to wounded soldiers during a war. Because of her work hospitals were improved and the proper training of nurses began. She was called "the Lady with the Lamp". Who was she? F - - - - - - - N - - - - - - - - - -.

2. In 1666 the Great Fire of London destroyed a large part of the city. A famous architect was asked to design a new London. He built St Paul's Cathedral and fifty-two other churches. His name was S - - C - - - - - - - - - - W - - -.

3. The English troops were attacking the town of Quebec. At night they climbed the Heights of Abraham and caught the French army unawares. The general in charge of the English was J - - - - W - - - -.

*Florence Nightingale*

# Place Names

Another way of distinguishing people was by mentioning where they lived. Simon who lived on the hill became Simon Hill, while Simon who lived by the village green, where the geese fed and the Maypole was put up for the Mayday festivities, was Simon Green.

In the same way we have the names Wood, Greenwood, Greenhill, Marsh, Lane, Heath, Dale and Glenn. Cornfield, Ditchfield, Dyke, Grove, Falconbridge, Poole, Rushton, Rushford, Underwood and Orchard all suggest to us where the owners of these names lived. So do Blackwell, Barnwell, Thorndyke, North, Northwood, Norgrove, West, Brook and Brooke, Byfield, Bythesea, Bythewater and Byteway.

About a thousand years ago our land was very different from what it is now. Most of England was covered with forests, woods, heathland and marshes. Bears, wolves and wild boars infested the forests and deer and wild cattle roamed about the land. There were few villages and towns and communication between places was very difficult, if not impossible.

Many tree names are found in these place names, which is not surprising when there were so many of them about and the wood was so necessary for building houses, making furniture, wagons, farm tools and for fuel.

The wood of ash trees was used for carts and ploughs, that of the hazel for forks. The long bows used by the English bowmen were made from the wood of yew trees, though rowan, or mountain ash could be used for bows, too. The rowan was considered a holy tree and gave protection from witchcraft and magic. Holly trees are still planted in hedges to keep witches away.

The long, supple branches of the osier willow were made into baskets, as they still are. Bunches of birch twigs made brooms. The wooden ships of the Navy were made from the oak tree. Do you know the song which has a chorus which goes, "Heart of oak are our ships"? Oak wood was also used for church doors.

A few tree names are Birch and Beech, Oakley and Oakden, Eastwood, Atwood, Ashwood, Hazelwood, Ashwell. Crabtree and Crabmill are two more, 'crab' of course, means the crab apple. The name Rountree means 'the dweller by the rowan tree'.

'Er' at the end of a word meant a dweller, so Bridger and Brooker mean the dweller by the bridge and the brook. Brig is a word that means brook and comes in the name Briggs.

Brock is the old name for the badger and we find it in many names both of places and people. Brockbank, Brockhouse, Brockhurst, Brockway and Brocklehurst are only a few.

Coomb or combe is a little wooded valley; Dun means a fortified mound. You can find many names containing these words, look for some. As you know, a ford is a place where a river is shallow enough to be crossed by wading. Villages and towns sprang up at fords and the word comes into many names, Ford, Forde, Longford, Fordham, Gosford (goose ford), Cranford (meaning cranes ford) and so on. Somerford was a ford only used in the summer.

Garth means an enclosure or a yard. Shaw was a small wood. We get Shaw as a name and also joined with other words such as Henshaw, while Bradshaw was the broad wood.

A holm meant either an islet in the river, or the evergreen oak, hence the name Holmes. And you can see that Holmshaw would be a small oakwood, or an island on which grew evergreen oaks.

Hurst also meant a wood and we find the names Hurst, Buckhurst and others. Stead was a place and ham was a home, so Hampstand meant the home place, or homestead.

Ridge and Ridgeway suggest a home on the ridge of an upland, and col means black, so Coleridge could be someone who dwelt on a black ridge. But as a bare upland can also be called a down, we get Downe, Downes and Downham.

The word for meadow or pastureland is a lea, or ley; this gives us the names Lea, Lee, Leese and Leyland. Stanley was a stony lea, Langley the long lea and Bradley a broad lea. Morley was the moor lea or a clearing on a moor.

When a new part of waste land was taken and cultivated it was enclosed. Many endings of names show this.

'Ton' meaning a hedge, is a place surrounded by a hedge. Ashton, Weston, Norton, Sutton, Middleton or Milton were names of people living at the east, west, north, south and middle of such a place. There are Astington, Norrington, Uppington and Westington, and Barton was a barley field.

'Worth' was a protected place and comes in names like Bosworth and Worth.

'Stoke' was a place closed in with stakes. This often became Stow, a name we find as a surname. Bristol was originally Bristowe, meaning the place by a bridge. This again, is still found as a surname.

'Fold' was fenced in with felled trees, and 'burgh' or 'bury' meant a hidden place.

See how many names with these ending you can find.

Some place names end with 'by'; these, Sotheby, Easterby and Westoby, mean a man living south, east or west of the village.

The word 'peel' means a castle, it is still used in the north of England, and of course you have heard of John Peel.

March, or Mark, means a border, or boundary. The word market comes from the same root because markets were held on the border between two countries or shires. The boundary between England and Wales was called the Welsh Marches.

Underwood, Smallwood, Littlewood, Townsend and Underhill are names which need no explanation.

An old Scotch word 'haugh' meant a meadow, or flat land by a river, so John Greenhaugh lived by a river in a green, grassy field. Wilfred Ferneyhaugh apparently dwelt in, or by, a riverside meadow where ferns flourished.

*A Wool Merchant*

*Sir Robert Peel*

When the big fairs we talked about earlier were founded, wool was the chief export from Britain to Europe. A word for a market was staple and the rich wool merchants were known as the Merchants of the Staple. We find the name Stapleton, Staples and Stapleford.

The names Newman or Newcome suggest new arrivals, and French, Scott, German, Welshman or Welch were given to people who came from France, Scotland, Germany and Wales. The name Welsh was also used for any stranger wherever he happened to belong. The Scotch form of Welsh is Wallace, and its other forms Wallis, Willis and Wales.

The names of priests were changed every time they moved to a new living, that is, were put in charge of a different parish. This must have been very confusing for them and their friends.

You will find that there are many persons whose surnames are the same as the name of a village, town or country, and they must have got those names from their homes. A very short list is Kent, London, Halifax, Hastings, Cheshire, Essex, Ireland, Holland, Dudley and Holloway.

The largest number of surnames in England are place names, and I am sure you will find many more among your friends.

### Famous Names

You have all heard of Sir Alexander Fleming, the discoverer of penicillin. The name Fleming means a man from Flanders.

Sir Robert Peel was a fine statesman. After a very bad harvest he repealed the Corn Laws which had made the price of corn very high. This made Peel unpopular with many of his friends, but it enabled poor people to get cheaper food. Another thing Peel did was to found our Police Force. From his name policemen got the nicknames 'Peelers' and 'Bobbies'.

Two other very famous statesmen were father and son. They were William Pitt the Elder, who was afterwards made Earl of Chatham, and his second son, William Pitt the Younger. Their name means a dweller by a pit or hollow.

Benjamin Britten is a modern composer who is very well known. You have no doubt heard his *Young Persons' Guide to the Orchestra* and the opera he wrote for children. It is called *Let's Do an Opera* and tells the story of a little sweep called Sam.

Two more musicians were Sir Edward German and John Ireland. German wrote very tuneful light operas, the favourite is *Merrie England*. Ireland is best known for his songs.

Two great writers were Sir Walter Scott and John Milton. Walter Scott wrote a large number of historical novels. If you are fond of history you will like many of his books and poems. Milton (1608–1674) held an important position in Cromwell's government. He became blind but that did not stop him making poetry, even though he had to dictate his poems to his daughter.

More poets were Robert Bridges, Rupert Brooke and Samuel Taylor Coleridge.

We have mentioned James Watt before. Once he was asked to mend an engine invented by a man called Newcomen, the 'en' at the end of this name is the same as 'er'. Watts studied the machine carefully and found some faults. He corrected these and improved the engine in many ways.

A great president of the United States of America was

*Abraham Lincoln*

*S - - I - - - - N - - - - -*

Abraham Lincoln. In 1863 he freed the slaves, an act for which he will always be remembered,

Until 1840 letters were charged for according to the distance they were carried. Rowland Hill suggested that all letters should cost the same, one penny, and that a stamp should be put on each envelope to show that the penny had been paid. His idea was carried out and the penny postage lasted until the 1914–18 war. If you happen to live in Kidderminster you know this already, for Rowland Hill lived there and there is a statue of him in the town.

## Puzzles for You

1. This man was a naval officer who later led two expeditions to the Antarctic. On the second, he and his companions reached the South Pole, but found that a Norwegian had got there first. On the return journey they were overcome by a blizzard and died. Who was he? R - - - - - F - - - - - S - - - -.

2. He was a Scotsman who went to Africa as a medical missionary. He explored many parts of Africa including the Victoria Falls and Lake Tanganyika. His name means black. He was found by another explorer but refused to return home. He was D - - - - L - - - - - - - - - -, and the man who found him was S - - H - - - - S - - - - - -.

3. This man was one of the greatest scientists and mathematicians of all time. Even as a boy he liked to make mechanical things. He made a windmill and put it on the roof of the house, and he made a treadmill for his pet mouse. Among many other things he discovered the law. of gravity and that light is really made up of many colours His name was S - - I - - - - N - - - - -.

# Alternative Origins

It often happened that a name might have more than one meaning. Take the names Bull and Peacock. They might be nicknames, or they may have been given to the owners of inns with the sign of a bull or peacock. And, by the way, Peacock was often changed to Pocock. Other animal and bird names may have come from inn signs.

Green may be a place name of someone living on the village green, or the owner may have played the part of Jack-in-the-green on Maydays, and as he was still called by that name after Maytime was past, it stuck to him and became his own.

The name Lowe may have been a nickname for a short man, an animal name from the French word loup, meaning wolf, or it may be a short form of Laurence. It was quite possible for three different men living in different places to acquire the same name, but for different reasons.

There are two possible origins for the great name Churchill. It may be a straightforward place name, someone who lived on the church hill. But some people think it comes from a French name de Courcelle. Either or both can be correct.

We have seen that Pollack, or Pollock, is usually little Paul, but it could sometimes mean the Pole.

Drake may have been a bird name or it may have come from a Scandinavian name 'draca', meaning dragon. The last meaning would certainly have suited Sir Francis Drake better, wouldn't it?

So you see tracing names is not always easy, but it is always fun.

*Sir Francis Drake*

35

## How Words and Names Altered

Many, many of our surnames are difficult to identify for they have changed such a great deal since they were first used. This was often caused by a misunderstanding, or by not hearing the word properly, or confusing it with another word. I'll give you a few examples showing how some of our words have changed.

An adder and an apron were originally a nadder and a napron, and an umpire was a noumper. But people confused these words with others beginning with vowels and the 'n' got in the wrong place. Sometimes it worked the other way round; what we call a newt was an ewt and a nickname was an eke-name. Eke means added, or also. A nickname is one that is added.

Surnames like Nash and Noakes were once 'atten ash' meaning at the ash, and 'atten oaks', at the oaks. The 'atte' has been dropped and the 'n' joined to the last word. The same change gives us Attlee from 'atte lea'. We still, however, find the names Atterway, Attenbury and Attenborough.

The letters 'm' and 'n' were often mixed up. A bishop who lived in Tudor times was called Latimer, which was really Latiner, a good name for a bishop.

Vowels in a word were easily changed so that we get Stanley meaning a stony lea, Standish, a stony pasture, Shipley and Shiplea, both meaning sheep meadow. Charlesworth and Charlton mean the enclosure of the churls. Do you remember what a churl was? If not, you had better look back.

Another strange thing is the way the letter 'p' often got into a word for no reason at all. We find Simpson for the son of Simon, Thompson for the son of Thomas, and Hampstead which should be Hamstead, or Homestead.

*A Tudor Bishop*

Often the final 'e' of a word was dropped, giving names like Swinburn, meaning swine (pigs) burn, or brook.

Many swine were kept in olden times. The children had the task of driving them into the woods where they fed on acorns and beech mast. So we find many names beginning with Swin or Swine. Two examples are Swinbank and Swinford, a ford suitable for swine to cross. Whitsunday really means White Sunday, and in the same way Whitfield and Whitmore mean Whitefield and Whitemoor.

Sometimes whole syllables were left out and Debenham became Deadman and Dedman, and Tuddenham was shortened to Tudman.

All this makes the study of names rather difficult and even experts do not always agree on the meanings.

If our ancestors altered simple words so much you will not be surprised at what happened to the names of people from other countries. We will look at some of these foreign names in the next section.

## Names of Foreign Origin

You will have learnt in your history lessons that our country was invaded by the Romans, the Danes or Norsemen, the Angles, Jutes and Saxons, and the Normans. Each of these invasions added to our language, and just as English contains Latin, Danish, Anglo-Saxon and Norman-French words, so many of our surnames came originally from these invaders.

There are not many Roman names, but here are a few. The Latin word for a camp was 'castra' which has become chester, caster and cester. You will find a lot of names ending with these words, Chester, Lancaster, Manchester and others.

'Strata' meant a paved road; now we say street. In names of places it can be strat as in Stratford, stret as in Stretton, or streat as in Streatham.

The name Britain comes from a Celtic word 'brit' which meant painted, because the British used woad to colour their bodies. This was to frighten their enemies in battle.

After the Angles and Saxons settled here the land was known as Angleland and you can see how that changed into England.

The Saxons got their name from the short sword used by their warriors which was called 'seaxe'. Sussex means the land of the South Saxons and Essex the land of the East Saxons. Norfolk and Suffolk are the lands of the North folk and the South folk.

In the section on place names we found names ending in 'ton' and 'by'. These are Scandinavian, so is the ending 'son'.

The Norsemen, or Danes, believed in many gods, whom they said lived in Valhalla. The names of our weekdays come from the names of these Northern gods. The chief god was Odin, or Woden. His day, Woden's day has become Wednesday. Another god was Thor, his day is now Thursday. Tuesday comes from Tew's day, and Friday is the day of Freya or Frija, who was a goddess. Saturday was the day of Saturn. Now you know why some of these names are spelt as they are. The name Thoroughgood probably was once Thurgod.

Two chiefs of the Jutes were Hengist and Horsa. Both these names mean the same, horse. When Horsa died he was buried at a place that was afterwards called Horsestead. Perhaps the name Horsepool comes from Horsa.

The Norsemen not only invaded Britain they also went to France and settled on the Western coast. This became

*Thor*

known as the land of the Northmen, or Normandy. The name Norman just means Northman.

But there were other reasons apart from invasion which made people leave their own homes and come to our land. Henry I invited Flemings, who were weavers, to settle here and teach his people their craft.

At the beginning of James II's reign, French Protestants were being very badly treated in their own country, because of their religion, so they left their homes and many came to England. These Huguenots, as they were called, settled here and some of them manufactured silk. Many French people came here, too, in order to avoid being killed during the French Revolution, and in all these cases some different names were introduced.

To return to the Normans. The early Norman kings married French wives, and they, of course, brought with them ladies-in-waiting and courtiers, all of whom spoke Norman-French, which was the fashionable language at court. Anglo-Saxon was despised and left for the peasants. Gradually the two languages became one, using words from both.

French words seem to have been altered (or corrupted, as we call it) far more than those of any other language. They were somehow much harder for the Anglo-Saxons to pronounce—or at least that is usually considered the reason. But is that correct, I wonder? Was it perhaps, not that they cou!dn't but that they wouldn't say the names properly? Was it their Anglo-Saxon stubbornness and a desire to annoy their hated conquerors?

Whatever the reason, we have some names which have become so corrupted that they are hardly recognisable. There is a book which tells of a Frenchman who landed on the English coast. His name was a royal one, Bourbon. The people in the village where he lived changed it to Barebones. The story may not be true, but it does show how names can be altered.

Beecham was originally Beauchamp, Goose may have nothing to do with the bird but is a corruption of Guise. Does the name Bellamy come from bel ami (good friend) or Boonham from bon homme (good fellow)? Pettitt, too, was it once petit, the French for little?

We do know many names of French origin. A lot of them begin with de, which becomes d' in front of a vowel. But in common speech the d was joined on. So the names Damerell, Danvers, Dawnay, Disney and Doyley were once d'Amerell, d'Anvers, d'Aunai, d'Isney and d'Oyley, meaning the people from Anvers and so on. D'Allemagne, meaning a man from Germany has become Dalmain or Dolman.

Summerfield, which sounds quite an English name, may be a corruption of Somerville, Dangerfield was d'Angerville and Mullins comes from the French word moulin which means mill.

At the Battle of Hastings a minstrel of William's, called Taillefer rode in front singing a war song. Taillefer means 'cut iron', that is, a sword smith. Now, in English, it is Telfer.

De Brus has become Bruce, de Puset is now Pudsey while Grenville and Grenfell were once Grainville.

Place names, if of foreign origin, were very often corrupted. Bridges is perhaps a version of Bruges, Bullen or Boleyn came from Boulogne and Challis was Calais. Druce is from Dreux, Hawtrey is Hauterive and Dampier came from Dampierre. The famous name Cornwallis is a corruption of a French name meaning a man from Cornwall, and Morris might mean Moorish.

The poet Chaucer's name came from chausseur, the French for shoemaker and Purcell, the name of a musician, was from an old French word which meant little pig. The name Vicar is not derived from a clergyman as we might think, but from verrer, a glass maker.

There are a great number of examples of these names, far too many to quote here, but you may like the following little proof of our habit of changing names.

In the opening of the story of Robinson Crusoe, Daniel Defoe makes him say that his name was Robinson Kreutznoer, but 'by the usual corruption of words in England' it had become Crusoe.

I hope I have told you enough about names to make you want to find out more. It is a fascinating subject and one which is not yet complete. There is still a great deal more to be discovered about names and their beginnings. So perhaps, when you grow up, you may become an etymologist and add to our knowledge. That long word simply means a student of words.

If you have not found your own name in this book you may be able to put it into its right group and then work out its origin. If you still are not able to discover it, perhaps your local library will have a dictionary of surnames which you may consult.

# Index

43

Doughty *23*
Douglas *5*
Dove *24*
Downe *30*
Downes *30*
Downham *30*
Doyley *40*
Drake *35*
Drinkwater *25*
Druce *42*
Duckett *23*
Dudley *32*
Dyke *28*

Easterby *31*
Eastwood *29*
Edison *7*
Ericson *3*
Essex *32*

Fairfax *23*
Fairhead *23*
Fairweather *25*
Falconbridge *28*
Falconer *9*
Faraday *14*
Farrar *11*
Farrier *11*
Faulkner *9*
Ferguson *2*
Ferneyhaugh *31*
Ferriday *14*
Ferrier *11*
Fiddler *11*
Finch *24*
Fisher *14*
Fitzalan *4*
Fitzgerald *4*
Fitzpatrick *4*
Flecher *10*

Flecker *10*
Fleming *32*
Fletcher *10*
Flint *24*
Ford *30*
Forde *30*
Fordham *30*
Forester *11*
Forster *11*
Foster *11*
Founder *14*
Fowler *9*
Fox *24*
Franklin *16*, *19*
Freeman *16*
French *32*
Friar *10*
Fry *19*
Fryor *10*
Fuller *11*

Gardener *9*
Gardner *9*
Garth *30*
Gaunt *23*
Gay *26*
German *32*, *33*
Gibbon *5*, *7*
Gibbs *5*
Gibson *5*
Gilbert *5*
Gills *4*, *15*
Gillett *4*
Gilliand *4*
Gillot *4*
Gilpin *4*
Gilmour *4*
Girling *23*
Glenn *28*
Godeve *5*
Goldsmith *10*, *19*

Goose *40*
Goodbeer *25*
Goodchild *25*
Goodfellow *25*
Goodliffe *25*
Goodman *25*
Goodwill *25*
Goodwright *16*
Gosford *30*
Gosling *24*
Gotobed *25*
Governor *13*
Gray *26*
Grey *26*
Green *28*, *35*
Greenhaugh *31*
Greenhill *28*
Greenwood *28*
Gregson *3*
Grenfell *42*
Grenvill *42*
Groom *9*
Grove *28*

Hackett *23*
Haig *12*
Haigh *12*
Halifax *32*
Hammond *5*
Hampstead *30*, *36*
Hanson *3*
Hare *23*
Harefoot *23*
Harper *14*
Harris *15*
Harrison *3*
Harvey *5*, *6*
Hastings *32*
Hawk *24*

Hawker *9*
Hawkes *24*
Hawkins *24*, *27*
Hawtrey *42*
Hay *12*
Hayward *12*
Hazelwood *29*
Heath *28*
Henshaw *30*
Herd *9*
Hereward *12*
Hewitt *3*
Hewitson *3*
Hewlett *3*
Hewson *3*
Hibbert *5*
Higginson *3*
Hill *28*, *34*
Hillary *26*
Hind *14*
Hoarlock *23*
Hobson *3*
Hodd *24*
Hogg *24*
Holland *32*
Holloway *32*
Holmes *30*
Holmshaw *30*
Horlick *23*
Hornblower *14*
Horner *10*
Horsepool *38*
Hostler *11*
Howard *5*, *12*
Howett *3*
Hubert *5*
Hughes *3*
Huggett *3*
Hudson *3*, *7*
Hunt *9*, *20*

Hunter *9*
Hurst *30*
Husband *14*
Hutchinson *3*

Ibbotson *5*
Ireland *32*, *33*

Jacks *2*
Jackson *2*
Jake *2*
Jakes *2*
Janson *2*
Jellicoe *7*
Jenkinson *3*
Jenner *10*
Jennings *3*
Jocelyn *24*
Johns *2*, *15*
Johnson *2*
Joiner *10*
Jones *2*
Jonson *5*
Joyner *10*
Joyson *5*

Kent *32*
Kennedy *23*
Kings *15*
Kinson *5*
Knight *18*

Laing *22*
Lamb *24*, *26*
Lambert *12*
Lancaster *37*
Lander *11*
Lane *28*
Lang *22*
Langley *30*
Lark *24*
Larkin *24*